Stories From Branson's 76 Country Boulevard... and Places Nearby

by

Don Paul Pirwitz

Bloomington, IN   Milton Keynes, UK
authorHOUSE

AuthorHouse™
1663 Liberty Drive, Suite 200
Bloomington, IN 47403
www.authorhouse.com
Phone: 1-800-839-8640

AuthorHouse™ *UK Ltd.*
500 Avebury Boulevard
Central Milton Keynes, MK9 2BE
www.authorhouse.co.uk
Phone: 08001974150

© *2007 Don Paul Pirwitz. All rights reserved.*

No part of this book may be reproduced, stored in a retrieval system, or transmitted by any means without the written permission of the author.

First published by AuthorHouse 4/5/2007

ISBN: 978-1-4259-3677-8 (sc)
ISBN: 978-1-4259-3678-5 (hc)

Library of Congress Control Number: 2006906317

Printed in the United States of America
Bloomington, Indiana

This book is printed on acid-free paper.

ACKNOWLEDGEMENTS

Special thanks to ...

My wife Sharon, my greatest love and severest critic, for assuring me I could do this.

Mike Oatman and Mike Lynch, founders of Great Empire Broadcasting, for giving me the opportunity to come west and get to know the Ozarks.

Janet Ellis, Branson broadcaster and former english teacher, for her guidance.

Greg Brock, a trusted courier.

And ... the thousands of entertainers, servers, tour guides and others involved in Branson tourism for making the town such a wonderful place to visit and write about.

Table of Contents

ACKNOWLEDGEMENTS v
FOREWORD. ix
PRESLEY'S VISION 1
THE BALDKNOBBERS ... WHO CAME FIRST? 7
GRAND COUNTRY. 11
MOE BANDY AND THE NIGHT THE PRESIDENT
    CAME TO TOWN 15
THE HARD LUCK DINER 19
MICKEY GILLEY ... THE URBAN COWBOY'S
    BRANSON ADVENTURE. .23
THE TEXAS GOLD MINORS 29
HAPPY TRAILS. 33
THE HAYGOODS ... HAY! THESE GUYS ARE GOOD . . .37
CAJUN CONNECTION 41
THE OSMONDS 45
BUCK TRENT 49
JIM OWEN. 53
THE LAST HANK 57
JIM STAFFORD. 61
AMANDA. 65
AKA HOMER LEE 69
DOUG GABRIEL 73
DANNY EAKIN 77
YAKOV SMIRNOFF. 81
LEGENDS IN CONCERT 85
SHOJI TABUCHI 91
BOXCAR WILLIE 95

Don Paul Pirwitz

FOREWORD

It was a warm summer night in the Ozarks. As had become my custom, I was hosting Grand Country Saturday Night, a live 11 to midnight radio show at Branson's Grand Country Music Hall. I had strapped on my walkman and stepped out onto a concrete fire escape at the rear of the building to get a listener's perspective on the show.

The show's music director and steel guitar player, Danny Yancy, was being featured during a performance by one of the guests. As his instrument rang out across the Ozarks airwaves I surveyed the gleaming neon lights that lit up the landscape in what has become the Country Music Show Capitol of the World. It was a magic moment. I realized it was the fulfillment of a life-long dream.

I grew up in Irondequoit, New York, a suburb of Rochester. My first exposure to country music came via the network version of The Grand Ol' Opry. My dad told me we were listening to hillbilly music and what made it unique was that hillbilly bands didn't use horns. It was all done with stringed instruments, which was unusual in the big band era (of course, neither of us had yet heard of Bob Wills Texas Playboys and other western swing bands that featured horn sections).

At age 15 I found myself being drawn to country music. I would sit up late at night and listen to far away radio stations on the AM band through a hail of static. Elvis was catching on and I was discovering what the "billy" in rock-a-billy stood for. At night I would scan the dial listening to Wayne Raney (with his Talkin' Houn' Dawg harmonica) on WCKY in Cincinnati; Lee Moore, The Coffee Drinkin' Night Hawk from WWVA in Wheeling, West Virginia and, of course, The Grand Ol' Opry and Ernest Tubb's Midnight Jamboree on WSM in Nashville.

There were 3,500 students in the high school I attended but I think I was the only one who even knew what country music was. That made me different. My friends had parties where we would play records and dance. I would bring my Kitty Wells records. That didn't make me the most popular kid around.

At 16 I began dating a pretty blond girl who would later become my wife. On our first date we went to a country music show starring Jim Reeves, Marty Robbins and the Louvin Brothers (all now enshrined in the Country Music Hall of Fame). She stayed with me anyway.

In my mind I dreamed of places where country music was mainstream entertainment. Where good ol' boys and pretty little girls danced to the music of fiddles and steel guitars.

My career in broadcasting led me into country radio: First at WNYR in Rochester (where I was delighted to notice some of my high school friends coming to shows I would emcee), then to Philadelphia where I worked at The Rittenhouse Ranch ... WRCP. It was in Center City, just off Rittenhouse Square and right around the corner from the Mike Douglas syndicated TV show where I had the chance to meet many of the top stars of country music. The trail then made its way halfway across the continent to the Ozarks. I had made it. Although I had never been to the area before, I knew I was home.

I first came to Branson in the spring of 1972. It was still a small town tucked along the bank of Lake Taneycomo. The two laned Highway 76 curved its way along a ridge that ran west to Silver Dollar City. There were no other side roads and the only way in or out of town was through a four way stop at the intersection of what is now Business 65 and Highway 76 in downtown Branson.

At that point the town boasted a total of four shows: The Baldknobbers, Presleys, The Foggy River Boys and a theatre where the Starlight Theater now stands, on the north side of the highway just west of Presleys. It hosted a string of shows the names of which I can't recall. The three main shows were already drawing capacity crowds and 76 Highway became famous for its traffic jams. There were hotels, restaurants and craft malls scattered along the road.

The area was enjoying steady growth during the 70's and early 80's and then came what was discribed as "The Branson Boom". The Roy Clark Celebrity Theater and Lowes' Theater began booking major country music stars. Names like Tammy Wynette, Porter Wagoner, Conway Twitty, Roger Miller, Bill Anderson and Loretta Lynn lit up the marquees at the two showplaces.

Other stars who had tested the waters during one, two and three night stands decided to open their own theaters. Mel Tillis, Charley Pride, Willie Nelson, Merle Haggard, Wayne Newton, Tony Orlando, Moe Bandy, Mickey Gilley, Glen Campbell and Johnny Cash more or less took up residence in Branson.

A promoter began building Cash Country (now the Remington Theater) to house the Johnny Cash Show. Cash made several visits to the area to court the media and promote the enterprise. And then, the unthinkable happened: The promoter was unable to secure the financing to finish the project. Billboards had gone up. Tickets had been sold. There were stories of tour buses pulling into the sea of mud that surrounded the unfinished theater just to find nobody there.

There was the story about Willie Nelson's first show in Branson. He did the show he had done successfully on the road for years and walked off stage at its end. Then someone noticed that some in the audience were still in their seats, others were milling around the theater. Apparently thinking it was intermission, the fans were waiting for the second half to start. They had to be told: "That's it .... the show's over .... it's time to go home".

It soon became apparent to Branson's entertainer-newcomers that it wasn't good enough here to just do a concert .... people expected a show. Several of the big names left town. Others stayed, adding dancers, comedy and special effects.

In the midst of all this "60 Minutes" did a piece on Branson, network morning shows featured the town and millions were now aware of what was rapidly becoming known as "The Country Music Show Capital of the World". To promote its Country Music image, 76 Highway, once referred to as "the 76 strip", was officially renamed by Branson's Board of Alderman, "76 Country Boulevard".

The Herschend family (owners and operators of Silver dollar City) expanded their empire to include The 4,000 seat Grand Palace (to date the area's largest theater) with shows hosted by regulars Glen Campbell, Louise Mandrell and Kenny Rogers and superstar guests like Brooks and Dunn, Vince Gill and John Denver; The Showboat Branson Belle; Whitewater, a state-of-the-art water park and Dolly Parton's Dixie Stampede, a fast paced combination of horse show and dinner theater.

There was talk of Branson becoming "another Nashville". The comparison offended many of Branson's old timers and it just plain wasn't true. Although Branson has several quality recording studios, it has never challenged Music City U. S. A. as a recording mecca and Nashville has never quite matched Branson when it comes to live performances.

As the new millenium arrived many of the big names had left town. Some, like Tony Orlando, Johnny Lee, Barbara Fairchild and Jeannie Kendall (suriving member of the father/daughter duo The Kendalls) remained residents of the area while doing the bulk of their performances on the road. New shows dot the landscape with over 100 now featured mornings, afternoons and at night. And, for the first time in its history Branson is accessible via a four lane highway.

Today's Branson has expanded beyond just country music (although it still seems to be the mainstay of the entertainment menu). Andy Williams' Moon River Theater is one of the town's most successful venues, Russian comedian Yakov Smirnoff is a veteran Branson entertainer and shows now feature magic, comedy, Broadway show tunes, big band as well as classic rock and roll. Branson boasts more theater seats than Las Vegas or New York City's Broadway.

The town maintains a family friendly atmosphere and welcoming hospitality. Outlet shopping malls now draw nearly as many visitors as the shows and although new roads have eased traffic congestion there's still some serious gridlock Thanksgiving weekend as shoppers pour in to do their Christmas shopping.

Each November, The Veteran's Homecoming draws over 100,000 additional visitors. Classic car midnight "cruises" make select weekend nights come alive during the summer. During January, February and March the city's "Hot Winter Fun" promotion draws fans to the few shows that remain open in the winter months in an effort to make Branson a year round tourist destination.

The Presley's: Steve, Gary "Herkimer" and Lloyd.

PRESLEY'S VISION

I'm sure Country Music, or some form of it, has been a part of the Ozarks since white settlers first pushed across the Mississippi and into the hills of what are now Missouri and Arkansas.

The Branson area has drawn visitors from around the world beginning with the publication of Shepherd of the Hills and the discovery of Marvel Cave.

The Shepherd of the Hills pageant was being performed in Branson as early as 1926.

In the 50s, the Herschend family moved to the area from Chicago and opened a gift shop at the entrance to Marvel cave. Their enterprize would eventually expand into what is now Silver Dollar City.

But, in my mind, the beginning of what is now 76 Country Boulevard happened on a clear March morning in 1967 when Lloyd Presley pulled his fruit truck to the side of the road along 76 Highway and cast his eyes on the field to the south of the road. Presley told me once it was just full of "weeds and sprouts". He inquired about the land at Jones Hardware Store, the only structure on the north side of that stretch of the highway. It was for sale. He eventually formed a partnership with his son, Gary, Larry Drennon and his son, Dave. Within weeks a crude forerunner of what is now Presley's Jubilee had taken shape. Lloyd said they rushed to get the job done in time for the summer tourist season.

The original Presley theater had no permanent seats. The first seats were canvas lawn chairs that were set up to accomodate the number of guests each night. "That way we were always guaranteed a sellout," Presley told me. The canvas chairs proved to be a hazzard for some in the audience. They had been purchased second hand and weren't in the best of shape.

Occasionally, one would rip during the performance leaving a patron seated in it on the concrete floor.

Lloyd's son Steve, who plays drums on the family's show, remembers when the Presleys first moved to Branson. "I would ride my sled down some of the hills on 76 Highway. There was never any traffic on the road in the winter time."

One of the most interesting characters in the Branson entertainment community over the years was Windy Luttrell, better known as Sid Sharp. Gary Presley recalls, "Dad went for his Army physical during World War II. On the bus he heard a commotion somewhere behind him. People were laughing at someone and a bunch of guys ended up in a pile on the floor. It wasn't until several years later dad met Sid and found out he was at the center of what was going on."

Sid and Lloyd later became acquainted and began working together in 1948. "Sid was a singer and played steel guitar. They had a show on the radio in Springfield beginning in 1951. their group was called The Ozarks Playboys. They would play small places across the Ozarks and later went underground at Fantastic Caverns north of Springfield."

Gary recalls joining the show: "When I was 3 they let me come on and sing 'Rudolph the Red Nosed Reindeer'. Then when I was 13 or 14 they figured they needed some comedy. Lloyd Evans (a Springfield broadcaster who hosted the radio show) asked if I thought I could do it. I said 'yes'. I got some bib overalls from my grandpa and some glasses from my other grandpa and an old hat." The character Herkimer was born and became perhaps the best known comedian in Branson.

For decades the Presleys would take their show on the road between November and March. "We would go out on Thursdays, play that night Friday and Saturday and come home on Sunday. When we were out on the road Sid would tell jokes, take his teeth out and had a way of flapping his lips that made us all laugh. At some point we decided he would be more valuable doing comedy and that's what he did for the rest of his life.

"He would also clean up around the theater, move things around and do odd jobs. We never asked him to do it. He just loved to work."

Sid was also "goosey" ... easily spooked. "We would 'snake' him: Plant a rubber snake in his bunk. He was the brunt of many jokes when we were on the road. One time we decided to just leave him alone for a while. I could tell it bothered him. He kind of got to like it ... and expect it. There's one reason I'm glad he's in heaven ... I don't think there are any rubber snakes there."

Today, Presleys' bright red state-of-the-art theater stands as the centerpiece of Branson's 76 Country Boulevard. Lloyd and Gary's homes form the southern boundry of the theater's parking lot. Within a few yards are Steve's home and the homes of several of Lloyd's grandsons, now a part of the Presley show.

On a typical Spring, Summer or Autumn night, Lloyd (now in his 80s) strolls across the parking lot, drags his "dog-house" bass on stage and performs along side his sons, grandchildren and great grandchildren.

His wife, Bessie, takes her place in a reserved seat in the audience. She rarely misses a show and that's usually in favor of a St. Louis Cardinals game on the radio.

The Presleys' show is a fast paced mix of new-Country, Classic Country, Gospel and Comedy. Many of the brightly costumed cast members have been with the show for decades. In many ways it's reputed to be the best show to work for in Branson.

Don Paul Pirwitz

Within a few miles of the Presley complex are dozens of theaters housing over 100 shows, hotels, restaurants, shops and condominiums. Each year an estimated 7 million visitors make their way down 76 Country Boulevard past Lloyd's front door.

Over the years Lloyd's neighbors have included Wayne Newton, Willie Nelson, Johnny Cash, Merle Haggard, Bobby Vinton, Tony Orlando, Kenny Rogers, Mel Tillis and others too numerous to mention. Today marquees flash names like Moe Bandy, Mickey Gilley, Yakov Smirnoff, Andy Williams, Pam Tillis, The Oak Ridge Boys and others who, like the Presleys, have made their mark exclusively in the Branson show community.

Celebration City

The Baldknobbers in the early '60s. (left to right) Jim "Droopy Drawers" Mabe, Bill Mabe, Lyle "George Agernite" Mabe, Bob "Bobolink" Mabe, John Smith (sitting), Curt Williams and Howard Hale.

THE BALDKNOBBERS ... WHO CAME FIRST?

The question is often asked: Who came first the Presleys or the Baldknobbers?

Well, that depends on what you mean by "who came first ... and where?

Presleys were the first to build a theater on what is now 76 Country Boulevard.

However, before the first shovel of dirt was turned for the Presleys' Theater, four brothers were making music in Downtown Branson.

The Mabes: Bob (Bob-o-link), Bill, Jim (Droopy Drawers) and Lyle (George Agernite) put together the Baldknobbers, named after a vigilante gang that roamed the Ozarks Hills following the Civil War. Their music was pure Hillbilly ... without apology. Bob played guitar, Bill was featured on dobro, Jim scratched the washboard (not just for the novelty of it but as a legitimate percussion instrument), Lyle thumped the washtub bass and their friend Chick Allen played the jawbone of a mule. Jim and Lyle's characters provided cornball comedy, often interupting more legitimate entertainers on the show.

Lyle Mabe remembers their first performances in a building that housed both Branson City Hall and The American Legion. "We played to about 50 people. Then we moved to the Sammy Lane Pavilion. It held about 300. Then we moved to the skating rink where we played to about 600. In 1968 we moved to our own theater."

Former long-time Baldkobber manager, Max Tate, tells of the early days: Cruising campgrounds and other gathering places in a sedan with a speaker on the roof and members of the group urging Branson visitors to come to the show.

Featured vocalist Gene Dove remembers coming on board in the late 70s. "Things were different then. The show was more centered on comedy. Jim and Lyle were on stage throughout the show. It was difficult at first. I'd be doing a serious love song while they were cutting up somewhere else on stage. After a while I got used to it.

"The lights and sound were a lot less sophisticated. We just had simple track lights on stage. They were on and that was it. Howard Hale, our piano player, would run sound from on stage with a sound board set up next to his piano."

Unlike today, the winter months featured road trips. "We would perform in Minnesota and Michigan. I had a hard time understanding those people when they talked. Next thing you know we'd be in south Louisianna and Texas where folks had an altogether different type accent and lifestyle. It was real culture shock."

There were some real high points on the road. "We once played a show with the Presleys and Foggy River Boys in The Mabee Center in Tulsa. They told me there were between 12 and 14 thousand people in the audience." In Omaha, the Baldknobbers would often draw bigger crowds than some major stars whose shows were scheduled during the same week, among them Ronnie Milsap, Dove's idol Ray Price and Michael Martin Murphy.

"It was fun getting out to meet the folks on the road but it was hard work. This was before roadies and we would have to carry our own equipment, set it up and tear it down after the show. I don't think I could do that today."

I was told one time that the brothers agreed there would be no nepotism in the Baldknobbers' organization, that their offspring would not have a part in the show. Although the firmness of the policy has come into question, several members of the next generation of Mabes and several of their friends decided to do their own thing. Dennis and Brent Mabe, Tonya Bilyeu along with friends Ed Snowden, Mike Gates and Jeff Tate formed their own group: Southern Exit. The group played across the Ozarks in talent contests, night clubs and other small venues. Bass player Brent Mabe comments: "If someone wanted a band to open an envelope ... we'd be there. Then they invited us to play at the 1984 Baldknobbers Christmas Party at the Holiday Inn. When they heard us play they reconsidered their policy. They saw we were serious and felt we had a decent amount of talent."

Eventually, all of Southern Exit, except for Mike Gates, would make their way to the Baldknobbers' stage. Tonya Allen left the show after a few years to become one of Mel Tillis' Stutterettes ... his backup singers.

Today the Baldknobbers play in a fancy 1500 seat theater with an elegantly decorated lobby and state of the art lighting and sound. But the show hasn't lost any of its down home hillbilly appeal. Tim Mabe has succeeded his late father Jim as Droopy Drawers Jr. and along with Stub Meadows continues the long traditon of cornball comedy.

The beginning of the 2006 season saw a third generation of Mabes become a part of the family enterprise. A vocal trio made up of Brandon (son of Tim Mabe), Denton and Garrett Mabe (sons of Dennis) took their place along side of their fathers on the Baldknobbers' stage. The addition coincided with the return of the trio's cousin Joy Bilyeu who had been a part of the show several year's earlier.

Days after the opening of the season, 48 year old Dennis Mabe, one of the first of the second generation of Mabes on the show, died suddenly following hospitalization for a heart ailment.

Venus and Glenn Robinson

GRAND COUNTRY

In 1971, Glenn Robinson drove his pickup truck onto the parking lot of what was becoming the Wal-Mart store on the north side of Highway 76 in Branson and began selling pottery and other items he had brought up from Mexico.

"They hadn't even turned on the electricity to the lights in the lot yet", he recalls.

Today, Grand Country Square includes a 319 room hotel, indoor water park, indoor mini golf, Grand Country Buffet, Grand Country Music Hall theatre, an arcade, a pizza buffet, custard stand, several retail shops along with the world's largest fiddle and the world's largest banjo.

"In 1972, we moved our business from the pickup truck to a tent. The next year we moved into a shop in what is now the two-story building at the front. Late in 1986, we bought the building housing Wal-Mart, remodeled and added Grand Country Music Hall, Indoor Mini Golf, and the Bonanza Family Restaurant ... it became the biggest Bonanza in the world."

One of the major breaks for Branson and Grand Country came in the early 90's when the CBS News show "60 Minutes" did a segment on Branson. They did it in the middle of winter. Tourists flooded into town and found they had little to do there at that time of year. Almost all of the shows, attractions, restaurants and shops were closed. Grand Country was just about the only game in town.

That year business in Branson jumped 20 percent ... mostly due to the large increase of first time visitors.

"I made a big mistake back then," Robinson admits. "I was still selling my hotel rooms for $30.00 a night. I was sold out every night. I should have raised my rates but didn't. Loretta Lynn and her husband stayed with us several nights."

Country music's biggest stars and millions of fans were finding out about Branson.

Glenn Robinson has definitely become one of Branson's greatest innovators. When the season traditionally began on Easter weekend and ended on the last day of October, he alone decided to do business year round.

"Several years before the '60 Minutes' piece, five business owners got together and decided to promote Ozark Mountain Christmas. We did it mostly by ourselves for two years, then Silver Dollar City committed to a 3 year run in opening at Christmas time."

"Our lowest point probably came during the 'Branson Boom.' It led to an excess of building and opening of new businesses. To help us determine our future, we participated in a study with some consultants to analyze how our business fit with Branson as a tourist destination. Along with importance of music for Branson, we discovered the need for our business to be more family friendly. This began the conversion of the 76 Mall Complex to the Grand Country Square as the home of the World's Largest Banjo, Fiddle, and Splash Country Indoors ... Missouri's first indoor Waterpark.

"Too often we don't consider tourist, as potential repeat customers. We just want to get as much as we can out of them while they're here and let them go their way. That doesn't work for us. We want them to tell friends back home what a great time they had, and we want them to come back."

To accomplish his goals - he has a staff of over 250.

"We have many employees who have been with us over two decades. Some have been here since we bought our first property in Branson."

His favorite part of the business?

"It has to be retail. When I was in high school, I would work... sometimes over 40 hours a week... in a grocery store. I used to enjoy seeing customers come back day after day. I went to college and got my Masters in Microbiology - but I didn't really want to do that. So I returned to retail."

Most of the planning for the enterprise is done by Glenn, his wife Venus, and their two daughters Debra and Jennifer.

"We have a basic philosophy: remember what didn't work, expand on what is working - once we arrive at a plan, move ahead and never look back."

Moe Bandy

MOE BANDY AND THE NIGHT THE PRESIDENT CAME TO TOWN

Moe Bandy has been a part of the Branson music community for nearly two decades and was instrumental in bringing the most distinguished guest ever to Branson..

He first came to town for a limited engagment at a rodeo in an arena where Celebration City now stands. He was so taken with the town that on his return to his home in San Antonio he packed his family into his van and drove back to the Ozarks, this time as a tourist. It took several years but eventually his name lit up the marquee on what had been The Plummer Family Theater on 76 Country Boulevard.

I think of Moe's career as having three phases. Honky Tonk Moe, characterized by his initial hits by songs that fit the whisky drinkin', smoke filled bar, cheatin', country-music-on-the-jukebox lifestyle ("I Just Started Hatin' Cheatin' Songs Today", I Cheated Her Right Out of Me" and "Hank Williams You Wrote My Life"). He was so strongly associated with the genre that the Texas legislature once named him "King of the Honky Tonks". Then there was Rodeo Moe with hit songs about rodeos and the cowboy lifestyle ("Bandy the Rodeo Clown", "Someday Soon", etc.). And then, Americana Moe featuring songs that spoke to the day to day life of Middle America.

One of Moe's best known hits is "Bandy The Rodeo Clown". The song was presented to him by way of a late night phone call from Country Music Hall-of-Famer Lefty Frizzell. Lefty had just written the song with super songwriter Whitey Shaffer. Despite what the song suggests Moe is quick to admit he never was a rodeo clown although he did ride a few bulls before coming to his senses and realizing it was easier and safer to sing country music. "I do have guys come up to me every once in a while and say 'Boy, you saved my life once out in Cheyenne'" Moe

Don Paul Pirwitz

recalls. "There's often no way to convince them I was never a clown so usually I just say ... 'Well, pardner, it was my job and I did the best I could'".

One of Moe's biggest fans is former President George Bush. Moe's hit "Americana" was used as the theme of one of Bush's presidential campaigns. In a televised tour of the White House conducted by Barbara Bush, the First Lady began in the Lincoln Bedroom and mentioned this was where Moe Bandy slept when he visited the Presidential Mansion. During one visit, Moe, the President along with golf champions Lee Trevino and Doug Sanders strolled out onto the front lawn of the White House. Several tourists were standing along the fence. One of them pointed to the four and shouted to the others, "Look ... there's Moe Bandy!"

Moe remembers a night in 1992 at Camp David when he and his daughter were dining with the president. "He said, 'Moe, tell me about this Branson place'. Later I got to sing 'Americana' at the Republican National Convention. The next day the President came to Branson. There was a rally at Silver Dollar City and then he came to my show. After the show he took a few minutes and spoke to the audience. It was a great thrill. There was a lot of security, too. They had guards stationed on the roof and all around the theater."

Bandy has also been a guest of the President at his home in Maine. There Bush finds great peace in just "sitting by the sea". During a particularly hard time in Moe's life, when his mother died and other personal problems we overtaking him, an invitation came from the ex-Chief Executive. It read: "Moe, you need to come up and sit by the sea for a while".

Celebration City

Debbie Kaye

THE HARD LUCK DINER

If there was a Hall of Fame for waitresses blond haired Debbie Kaye would unboubtedly be enshrined there.

Debbie is one of the singing servers at the Hard Luck Diner, a 50's themed malt shop in The Grand Village on 76 Country Boulevard. "My first job was working at my parents truck stop: Chef Rudy's along Interstate 90 in Kimball, South Dakota. Except for working as assistant to the band director in college my career has always involved food service," she admits.

During a trip to Nashville she made a tape at The Barbara Mandrell Museum singing to a Karaoke track. Her parents were so impressed they invited her to sing at the grand opening of of their new truck stop. Arming herself with hundreds of tracks she began her musical career. Later she toured with her own band, playing small gigs, mainly in Iowa.

"I took a lot of inspiration from Marie Osmond. I first saw her after her divorce and realized that she, like me, was a single mom. So was the recently widowed Lorrie Morgan. I figured if they could do it ... I could, too. Of course, I didn't stop to think that they could afford nannies and I couldn't."

"I first came to Branson in 1993. I came here three times that year. The third time I auditioned for a part in 'Pump Boys and Dinettes'." She didn't get the job. "But I did get some advice. Someone told me 'If you want to get on a show in Branson, move here'." She did. Working as a waitress she continued to audtion for shows. After two and a half years and six auditions for "Pump Boys and Dinettes" she got the job, performing with Maggie LeMee as one of the Cupp sisters, singing waitresses in a small cafe set in a mythical town in North Carolina. "We not only sang but we also were featured on percussion ... wooden spoons, pots, pans, colanders ... anything you might find around the kitchen."

Don Paul Pirwitz

Today Debbie's typical day begins when her alarm sounds at 6:15. By 7:30 she's enjoying breakfast at (where else) The Hard Luck Diner. "I'm particularly fond of the three egg omelet. sometimes I just settle for bacon and eggs. The rest of the day is usually a blur, waiting tables, singing to customers and selling copies of my albums. Today we had 18 buses come in," she told me recently, "But it's always fun. I get to work with some really talented people. There aren't many rules. For the most part we're free to do whatever we think will be the most fun for our customers."

The walls of the diner are covered with memorabilia that recall the 50's and feature personal items from some of the big stars of the past decades: Brenda Lee, Dolly Parton and Mickey Gilley to name just a few. "I grew up watching Buck Trent on 'Hee Haw' and it's always a thrill when he shows up."

And you never know who might show up at the diner. Singing server Montana West loves to sing the 1968 hit "Harper Valley P. T. A.". One time, without knowing it, she found herself singing it to Jeannie C. Riley, the vocalist who made it a hit. Another time she picked a man out of the audience, looked him in the eye and delivered the line "Mr. Baker tell me why your secretary had to leave this town ...". She didn't know his name really was Baker .... well, Bakker. It was televangelist Jim Bakker. He took it well and everyone had a good laugh.

Showboat Branson Belle

Mickey Gilley

MICKEY GILLEY ... THE URBAN COWBOY'S BRANSON ADVENTURE

Mickey Gilley has had the advantage of being at the right place at the right time at least twice.

When the movie "Urban Cowboy" needed a setting it was Gilley's Houston area nightclub that was selected. The movie and associated hit records not only had an impact on the Country Music record charts and American culture in general, it also created an entire era in Country Music history.

When Branson began to boom, Mickey Gilley was one of the first national stars to get on board, even though he was reluctant to do so. "I looked at my schedule," He recalls, "and noticed I was booked for six shows on a Monday, Tuesday and Wednesday in Branson, Missouri. I'd never heard of the place. I hadn't had a hit record in a few years and I didn't want to go to the middle of nowhere and play to an empty house. I called my agent and told him to get me out of the date. He said all six shows were already sold out.

"Some time later I was talking with Mel Tillis who had already established a successful theater in town. He said 'Sell everything you have and move to Branson'."

It wasn't long before Gilley's name was on the marquee of what had been the Hee Haw Theater and later Bill and Janet Dailey's Country Music World.

Gilley's first two years in Branson saw a trio of setbacks and tragedies. At the end of the first year his Branson enterprise was in serious financial trouble.
"I went broke. When I took over the theater we had committed to several acts for limited engagements that just weren't paying off. My show was doing well but at the end of the year, after

paying the employees, paying the acts we'd committed to and other expenses we had no money for taxes, insurance and things." Gilley managed to work out a deal to get everyone paid off.

"Then there was the fire", he recalls. The blaze leveled the theater. Although insurance paid most of the cost of reconstruction, lost revenue insurance failed to adequately cover expenses that built up during the rebuilding period. Boxcar Willie to the rescue. America's Favorite Hobo had performed several times at Gilley's Texas nightclub.

"He wasn't doing matinees at his theater (right across the street) and I asked what it would cost to use his theater for afternoon shows. He said '50 cents a seat'. I said 'I'll pay you a dollar a seat'. We both came out ahead on the deal. In fact, I was doing two shows on Sundays and doing so well that when I left he started doing shows on Sunday."

Meanwhile, Conway Twitty, who had been doing matinees at Gilley's Theater, arranged to do an afternoon show across the street at The Jim Stafford Theater. One Friday afternoon after finishing his show at Stafford's, Conway left to return to his home in Nashville. On the bus between Branson and Ozark he became violently ill. Just north of Ozark an ambulance was summoned and he was rushed to Cox South Hospital in Springfield. Within hours he was dead from a burst anurism in his stomach.

"Conway and I went way back. When I had my first hit with 'Room Full of Roses' in 1974 I met with Conway. He was in his dressing room in a club. I told him I had done the song. He didn't seem to remember hearing it and then it came on the radio and he said 'Oh, that "Room Full of Roses".' He took an interest in me and took me on the road. I would open for him and would be introduced as 'Mickey Gilley and the Twitty

Birds (Conway's name for his band). I really hated the way that sounded.

"I had been on the road for some time with Conway and noticed he rarely spoke to me. It bothered me. I thought he didn't like me. I mentioned it to Big Joe, his bass player and MC. He said, 'Just go over and talk to him. He's just kind of shy and not very open.' I did. He opened up and we became close friends. I'm just sorry I never had the chance to say 'goodbye' to him and tell him how much he meant to me."

After the setbacks of his first two years, Mickey realized his show wasn't quite fitting in the way he wanted it to in Branson. "I went to Presleys and The Baldknobbers to see how it was done in Branson. I decided to do two things: Come on at the beginning of the show without an opening act and add some comedy."

Enter Joey Riley.

"Jim Owen had invited me to see his afternoon show at The Wildwood Flower (a supper club run by Bill and Janey Dailey). Jim was doing a bit where he was asking each band member to name his favorite cowboy. He went from one to another getting answers like 'Roy Rogers', 'Gene Autry', 'Hopalong Cassidy'. When he got to Joey ... who was playing steel guitar ... he just skipped him and went onto the next band member. Riley protested and asked 'What about my favorite cowboy?'. 'Well', Jim told him ... real seriously ... 'I figured you were too young to remember any of the great cowboys.' 'That ain't true!' he said. 'Then who is it?' ... and Joey said 'Roger Staubach'. I couldn't stop laughing."

After conferring with Owen, Gilley asked Riley if he wanted to do evenings on his show along with Owen's matinee. The answer was "yes" and Mickey had not only a new comedy star for his show but an outstanding steel guitar and fiddle player.

"Joey was doing great on the show but I noticed he was kind of holding back at times. I asked what was wrong. He told me some of the other cast members thought he was grabbing too much attention for himself. I told him what he was doing was good for the whole show and not to pay attention to what the others were saying."

Before long Mickey was sharing space on his billboard with Joey and gave his blessing when Riley decided to do his own matinee show at another theater.

Gilley regularly commutes from Branson to his home on 22 acres near Houston. To make the trip he pilots his own twin engine plane. One time while returning to Branson he overshot the runway at the Point Lookout airport south of town and skidded onto a pile of large rocks. He was able to walk away but the plane was severely damaged.

Although embarrassed, he soon introduced a new drink at the Gilley's Texas Cafe next to his theater. "I called it Gilley on the rocks with all proceeds going to replace my damaged aircraft."

I once mentioned how gracious he always seemed to be and lacking in the ego so often associated with stars of his caliber. "My cousin Jerry Lee (Lewis) got all the ego in the family. He once said his greatest regret is never having the chance to sit in the audience and watch himself perform."

Marvel Cave beneath Silver Dollar City

The Texas Gold Minors circa 1990

THE TEXAS GOLD MINORS

In the late 80s a group of teen and pre-teen entertainers was making its mark on the Opry circuit in Texas. Performing in small venues, The Texas Gold Minors had matured musically and were ready to make their next big step ... Texas honky tonks.

The idea didn't set well with the Gold Minors' parents. The group detoured and found a new home in Branson. Over the next two decades individual members of the group were to have a profound impact on the Branson entertainment community and Country Music in general.

The six original members moved into a large house on Fall Creek Road about a mile south of 76 Country Boulevard. Three of the moms would take turns supervising the youngsters in their new home.

"We really didn't have many problems, recalls redheaded Gold Minors fiddler Nancy Henson. "We all knew what we wanted to do and that goal kept us on track. It was nice. We had a pool and many nights we would jam into the wee small hours with other young Branson entertainers like Greg and Scott Presley"(grandsons of Lloyd).

Gary Myers, a veteran Branson entertainer and guitar player for Mickey Gilley, took time to coach the young entertainers. Nancy Henson remembers, "He taught us an audience will 'hear what they see'. That is, our visiual impact will enhance the sound of our music. Up until then we had concentrated only on our music and not our stage presence. To this day I always drop to my knees when I play 'Orange Blossom Special'."

Aside from Nancy, the original group was made up of Vocalist Kelly Jackson, her brother Michael on drums, Wyatt Beard on

Don Paul Pirwitz

keyboards, Guitarist Brian Spradlin, Bass-man and vocalist Clay Cooper and singer Erica Bussey.

Later the group would add steel guitar player Joey Riley, another veteran of the Texas Opry circuit, along with comedian Paul Harris from Mountain View, Arkansas. "I wasn't really from Texas like the rest," Harris admits, "but they changed the rules for me."

Later Minnesota fiddler Bruce Hoffman was allowed to join the group along with guitar picker John Conley.

What ever became of the Texas Gold Minors?

Nancy Henson fiddled on The Ray Stevens Show during his two tours in Branson. In between she played for Country Music Hall-of-Famer Charley Pride. Today she produces personalized childrens albums.

Kelly Jackson is married and raising a family.

Her brother Michael performs on the road with Branson resident Tony Orlando.

Wyatt Beard is now on the road with maga-award winning Country star Kenny Chesney.

Brian Spradlin performs with Country star Joe Nichols.

Clay Cooper performed on Country Tonight and now headlines his own show, The Clay Cooper Country Music Express.

Erica Bussey has moved to Nashville where she works days as a dental assistant and nights with her band in lower Broadway.

Blacksmith Shop at Silver Dollar City

Roy Rogers, Dale Evans and "Dusty" Roy Rogers Jr.

HAPPY TRAILS

In 2003 an American landmark was moved 2000 miles from California to Branson.

The Roy Rogers/Dale Evans Museum in Victorville, California had seen a decreasing number of vistors after the Interstate Highway caused traffic to bypass its location.

Roy Rogers Jr., known to his friends as Dusty, had been to Branson several times, "I did shows with Boxcar Willie and The Sons of the Pioneers and in 1998, after dad died, I thought mom needed to get away from California for a while. So we brought her to Branson. She loved it here. Most of the shows, when they found out she was coming, put 'Welcome Dale' on their marquees. She really appreciated the hospitality. On the way home she told me 'If anything should happen to me, consider moving the museum to Branson'. Two years later we took a serious look at moving. The City of Branson sent Mike Rankin and several other folks out to California. They made a presentation and pretty much convinced us we needed to be in Branson. We considered getting mom a condominium here but her health was declining and it just wasn't possible."

The new facility was built (literally) by Dusty Rogers. A former general contractor, he supervised the contruction of the museum, gift shop and new Happy Trails Theater. The museum features over 35,000 pieces of Rogers memorabelia including Roy's horse Trigger, Trigger Jr., Dale's horse Buttermilk and the family dog Bullet mounted in a display case. Another display is one of Dusty's favorites: "Back in Ohio, before they moved to the west coast, my dad and grandpa were going to build a house. They didn't have much money so they built a device ... a board about two feet long with a horseshoe shaped metal scoop that they wired to the coil on their old Model T. It produced an electromagnetic field, they would drag it through the streets of town and it would attract metal objects, mainly nails, that they used for building. And, it still works. I've got it plugged in in the museum and nails still stick to it."

The theater features daily shows with Dusty and his band the High Riders. The show is more like a friendly visit with Dusty featuring songs that bring back fond memories of his mom and dad and stories of life in the Rogers family. Dusty is quick to remind the audience, "We don't do Country Music ... we do Western Music. There is a difference." Although the songs change from season to season there are several mainstays, one being the gospel standard "Wayfaring Stranger". "I guess the song goes back a ways but several years ago I heard it for the first time," Dusty recalls. "I went to my mom and told her I had heard this song. She asked me to sing it for her. I said 'I can't, I don't have my guitar'. She said, ' what difference does it make, you don't play guitar anyway, so just sing it for me now'. So I did. She just loved it and asked me to sing it on my show. Then she asked if I would sing it at her services when she 'graduated' from this earth. It was difficult but when she passed away I did it and now I do it on every show in honor of her."

The Happy Trails Theater is small by Branson standards and the stage barely rises above the level of the audience. The presentation is simple and free of high tech lighting, smoke or specials effects.

Although he may have been born with a silver spoon in his mouth, Dusty had a fairly down-to-earth upbringing and was taught to work for what he wanted. "When I was 16," he remembers, "I had my eye on a car and asked dad to help me buy it. "He said, 'I'll tell you what, you earn enough money to pay for half of it and I'll pay for the other half'. Well, I went out and worked hard at every little job I could find. I really wanted that car and it didn't take me long to get the money together for my half of the price. I went to tell dad I had raised my half of the price and he said, 'the deal's off'. I was crushed. Then he explained that he had gone out and bought the car for me already knowing I would raise my half of the money."

During a visit one time I asked Dusty if there was a special moment he recalled with his father. He told about driving him around the family's ranch in a truck one day.
"I knew he wouldn't be with us forever and I felt the need to tell him how much he meant to me. So I pulled the truck to the side of the road and said 'Dad, I just feel the need to tell you how much I love you.' We both sat there for a while by the side of the road with tears rolling down our faces."

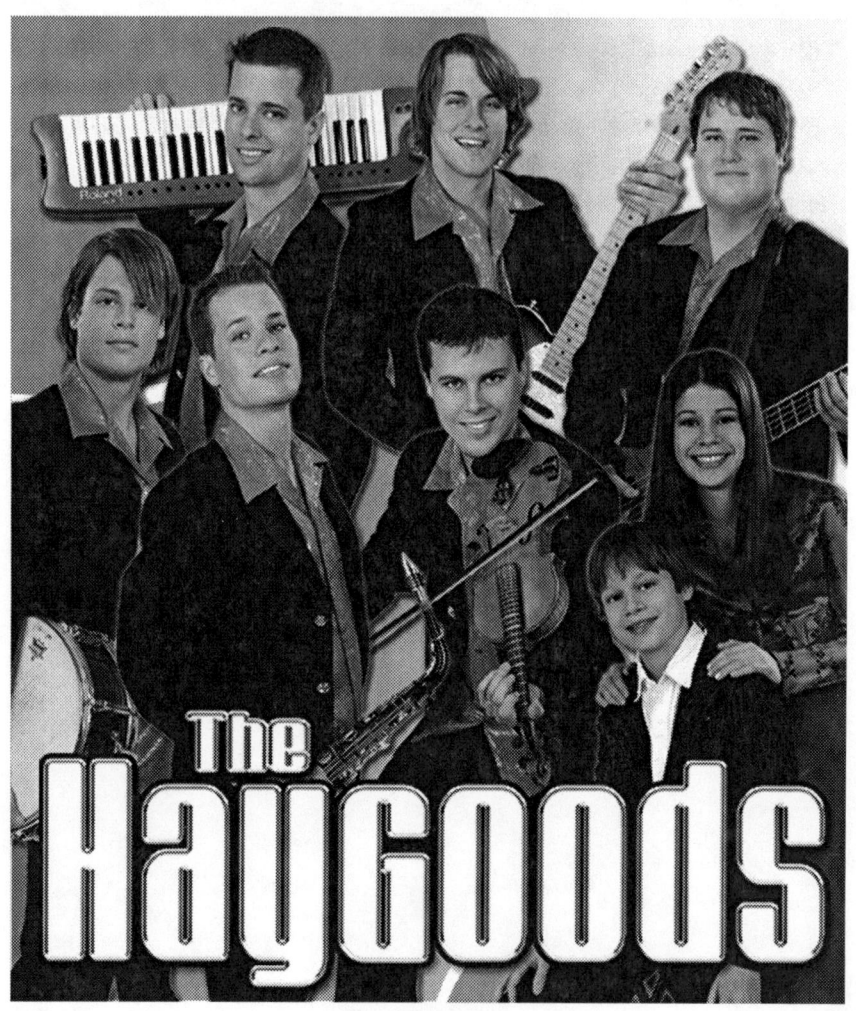

The Haygoods

THE HAYGOODS ... HAY! THESE GUYS ARE GOOD

The future of Branson may well rest with acts like The Haygoods. Although the show draws fans of all ages a survey would probably show an audience slightly younger than average for a Branson show.

This highly-charged combination of music, dance and daring acrobatics fills the stage at Music City Center. The cast is made up of seven brothers (Patrick, Timothy, Dominic, Sean, Michael, Matthew and Aaron) and their sister Katherine. They range in age from pre-teens to upper 20s..

The Haygoods' story begins in San Antonio where Jim Haygood was working in the redi-mix concrete industry. His wife Marie wanted oldest son Timothy to take music lessons. He selected the violin. At age 11, he had the opportunity to audition for Cajun fiddler Fiddlin' Frenchie Burke. Frenchie was impressed and offered to teach the young Haygood. Jim and Marie agreed so long as Burke agreed not to teach him any songs about barrooms, cheatin' or drinking.

When it came time for Patrick to take music lessons he was taken to a local music store where he picked out a set of bells. The bells led to drums, marimba and eventually keyboards.

As other siblings came of age they joined the family group which was soon on the road with Burke playing fiddle festivals and smaller venues around the state of Texas.

Before long the group was doing one-nighters around the state for over 100 dates a year.

And then, in the early 90s, two things happened: Jim and Marie saw the "60 Minutes" feature on Branson leading to a trip by

Don Paul Pirwitz

Jim to the the town and the group's appearance at a Cowboy Convention in Oklahoma City where they were seen by Silver Dollar City entertainment coordinator Rex Burdette.

Within days the Haygoods were offered a summer gig at Silver Dollar City. From 1993 to 2002 the family performed at the theme park, fine tuning their craft and adding new dimensions to their show each year. In 2003 they moved to their current home at Music City Centre.

Today's Haygoods Show is intense. It features a variety of music including Country, Pop, Big Band and Celtic. The dance numbers graduate into sometimes frightening acrobatics: Michael summersalting off the grand piano and landing on his feet while playing guitar and never missing a lick along with liberal use of trampolines and startling special effects. "We used to do a bit where we danced off the walls", Dominic recalls. "But we cut it out. It frightened too many people."

Many of the daring acrobatics were conceived of at home. "We had a trampoline beneath a second floor deck. We would practice diving off the deck onto the trampoline.
We recommend no one try this a home .... like we did."

Although the family harmonies ring out clearly during the show, all is not always harmony backstage. "We all love each other," Patrick comments, "But when you're with someone all the time, year after year, there are going to be some conflicts. Usually it's little things ... like someone hits a flat note during 'Amazing Grace'. We've smashed six or seven fiddles over the years and broken a number of bows. While we were at Silver Dollar City we had punched several holes in the walls of our dressing room. We covered them with posters and hoped no one would notice."

The world's largest fiddle at Grand Country Square

Cedric Benoit and Cajun Connection

CAJUN CONNECTION

A walk through Silver Dollar City is a treat for the senses. The look of the rustic turn-of-the-century buildings and costumes; the smells of coal and wood fires mixed with them blended aromas of barbecue, veggies and funnel cakes sizzling over open fires; and the sounds: The whistle of the steam train echoing through the woods, the delighted screams of guests experiencing the park's thrill rides and the music. The music is mainly native Ozarks hillbilly and gospel. But occassionally other sounds find their way into the mix ... the jagged rhythms and piercing strains of the fiddle and accordian, a music more native to an area hundreds of miles south of the Ozarks.

Cajun accordian player-singer-songwriter Cedric Benoit credits his Branson experience with helping him develop a unique musical presentation. He discribes his music as a "Blues-based-Zydaco-ish-Cajun blend. When I first came to Silver Dollar City I felt the need to perform in English, knowing that most of the folks I'd entertain didn't understand French. But then folks would come up from Louisiana and expect me to sing in French. So I was forced to become a bilingual entertainer."

Cedric's Cajun Connection Show is definately a high energy performance. During his second season at Silver Dollar City he is reputed to have come within a quarter of an inch of stomping a hole in the floor of the park's gazebo. " I still do a lot of stomping but I stomp a little softer in my older age. I only know one speed. Sometimes it's 100-degrees on our stage but we still give it all we've got. It's all about Gatoraid and salt tablets. I used to be a steel worker and a welder. I know what it's like to work really hard. These people come here and spend their hard earned to money to get into Silver Dollar City. We owe them nothing less than our best. Lot of people tell us it looks like every show is the first time we've been on stage. We always try to give 150 percent."

Don Paul Pirwitz

At age 4, Cedric remembers his first exposure to music: "It was Hank Williams. Then when I was 12, I got my first accordian. Sometime later I got inspired when I heard Doug Kershaw play 'Cajun Stripper'. It just knocked me out.

"Music is not what I do," he explains, "Music is what I am." Over the years he's written and recorded hundreds of songs and produced more albums than he can remember. "I want each song to be like a movie. I want to be able to take the music away and still have it say something that people can relate to."

One of the more colorful entertainers in Branson or anywhere for that matter is Cajun Connection's Washboard Leo. Leo Thomas, a native of Mandeville, Lousianna, got his musical start across Lake Poncetrain in the French Quarter of New Orleans as a piano player and drummer.

It was while performing at a folk festival in The Netherlands that he was introduced to the Washboard. "I was playing drums for a group that was invited to play at the festival. But they informed us since all the music at the festival was accoustic I couldn't play the drums. One of the guys in the band handed me a washboard. I played it about the same way I would play a drum set and it worked."

Leo moved from place to place, band to band, and ended up playing washboard in a Bluegrass group called Cornbread in Eureka Springs, Arkansas. "When that gig ended I came to Silver Dollar City and said 'I'm Washboard Leo and I'm looking for a job'. Before long I was playing in Cajun Connection with Cedric."

His washboard, which he has named Nadine, is far from the average hardware store variety washboard. It comes complete with cowbells, a block, special effects and a pickup so it can be plugged into an amplifier. "My dad made me about a hundred scrub boards ... the metal part in the middle of the washboard ... before he died. I go through a couple of them a year ... and my brother made me a special set of thimbles to cover my fingers. Originally I used regular thimbles but I kept wearing them out. The ones my brother made are made of heavy steel and they'll last forever."

A high point of his career was getting to play at the White House for President Bill Clinton's 50th birthday party. "When he was Governor of Arkansas I was playing drums and washboard at a club in Little Rock. He would bring his sax and sit in with us from time to time. His wife called us and asked if we would play for his party on the White House lawn. It was fun trying to get Nadine through Secret Service. They asked me to open the case and took a few steps back when they saw her. I think they thought it was a bomb."

ANNUAL EVENTS IN BRANSON

HOT WINTER FUN
January, February and March
An attempt to make Branson a more year round attraction with a limited number of shows and attractions staying open during the winter months.

WORLDFEST
April and May
A festival at Silver Dollar City featuring hundreds of entertainers of all kinds from all around the world.

BRANSONFEST
April
A festival previewing shows for the coming season.

KIDSFEST
June, July and August
A Silver Dollar City festival with hundreds of attractions for youngsters.

SHEPHERD'S SUPER SUMMER CRUISE
A massive classic car event featuring a midnight cruise, celebrity guests and special entertainment.

FESTIVAL OF AMERICAN MUSIC AND CRAFTSMANSHIP
September and October
A gathering at Silver Dollar City of hundreds of craftsmen and unique musicians from all around the country.

BRANSON VETERANS' HOMECOMING
November
A special weeklong tribute to America's veterans.

OZARK MOUNTAIN CHRISTMAS
November and December
Branson gets decked out for the holidays with special shows, lighting displays and shopping.

BRANSON ADORATION PARADE
First Sunday in December
One of the world's largest Christmas parades.

THE OSMONDS

The Osmonds have .... on and off ... been a part of the Branson music community since the early 90s.

The family moved to Branson at the urging of youngest brother Jimmy, most likely the business brains of the talented family. They set up shop in what was originally the Bob O' Links Theater on 76 Country Boulevard near Highway 165.

Jimmy first came to Branson as a real estate developer. "I worked on the Branson Meadows project and in the process found myself leasing a theater. I had planned to put Harry Blackstone Jr., the magician, in there but that didn't come together so I called the brothers. They were doing various things and agreed to come together and give it a try. Our first show was a sellout.

"Being in Branson gave me some great growing moments. I had been in show business my entire life but most big entertainers live life in a bubble surrounded by agents, managers, publicists and things. Being in Branson and actually operating a theater gave me a better look at the big picture. I had to deal with staff, even see that toilets got fixed. I got to know what kind of popcorn people liked best and I was able to meet a lot of our customers one-on-one and find out what they liked and didn't like about our show.

"One of the high points in our Branson experience was bringing Bob Hope to town. He and I were old golfing buddies and I had known him for a long time but having him sit in the audience and watch our show in Branson was really special.

"But our stay in Branson was exhausting and expensive. I decided we needed to do more than just come out and pick and grin. We added other acts and actually put in a skating rink on stage with skaters. I had to expain to my brothers that they were going to have to come out and sing on the ice. To justify the expense of it all we had to do two shows a day six days a week. It took a lot out of us. But working in one place most of the time added a lot of stability to our lives. I've been able to raise my kids in the same house so far."

Today Jimmy and his four brothers have gone separate ways. Occasionally they get together for special concerts, many of them in England and for the family Christmas show in Branson.

Few, if any, acts in music have experienced the amazing highs and lows the Osmonds have. Merrill remembers, "We made a lot of money, we lost a lot of money, we trusted some people we probably shouldn't have trusted. But it made us stronger as a family.

"The highest point may have been performing for and meeting Queen Elizabeth. Getting to meet Elvis was neat. How many people got to do that."

Brother Wayne remembers Madison Square Garden: "It was like a sea of flashbulbs going off. Girls screaming so loud we could hardly hear ourselves sing. It was a great feeling."

The worst gig? According to Merrill: "A rodeo in Montana. We had white suits and we were to be driven to the stage in the middle of the arena on an old buckboard. It had been raining and the wagon got bogged down in the mud. We had to walk the rest of the way to the stage and then we had no microphones. Then a bull got loose and cowboys had to get the bull out of the way while someone brought us our microphones."

"We were also the first act to use pyro-technics," Wayne recalls, "and we did it all ourselves ... with black powder. I loved to weld so I made little metal boxes to put the powder in. We would ignite them with flash bulbs. One night we put too much powder in a dish too near the drum set. When we set if off, it knocked Jay clear off his drum seat."

Jimmy remembers waking up one morning and seeing Good Morning America doing a piece on early Elvis impersonators. "They were holding up the cover of one of my albums. It kind of shocked me. But I guess I may have been the first Elvis impersonator. We were playing Las Vegas and Elvis intoduced us to the guy who made his costumes. We got costumes like his and I would go on and do 'I Got a Woman'. Sometimes Elvis would come by and watch me from the lighting booth. I could see him there and it was a strange feeling having him watch me imitating him."

One time I asked Merrill if he thought he had a normal childhood. "No. We're (the brothers) best friends. But we never had any friends outside the family. It was hard to meet girls we would want to date. I never had many of the normal teenage experiences, like getting beat up at school. I missed that."

Buck Trent

BUCK TRENT

For Buck Trent his first big break in show business came as a teenager playing on a television show in Asheville, North Carolina. "I played an hour a day with Cousin Wilbur and his wife, Blondie Brooks. On weekends we'd go out on the road and I made $40.00 a week. I thought I was rich.

"Wilbur was the one who taught me how to entertain. He said 'Buck, you can't just stand there and play. You've got to entertain people with that instrument. You can't just stand there and frown.' In Branson it's 75 per cent through the eyes that people are entertained. That's why we wear the bright clothes with the rhinestones and all ... and the band looks so good. Andy Williams told me the other day, he said, 'I've never seen a man change into so many jackets in one show.' That's what we do." During a typical show Buck changes outfits six or seven times. "There are people there who don't know us from Adam. We've got to make an impression. We've got to really entertain them so they remember they saw us. We do a high energy show. It's a regular fire drill."

Along the road from Asheville to Branson Buck Trent made many stops. Aside from being a flashy entertainer and outstanding picker he is also one of Country Music's great innovators. "When I went to Nashville in 1959, almost nobody was doing bluegrass and I couldn't buy a job playing banjo. So, I came up with the idea of electrifying the five-string banjo so I could play something other than bluegrass. Bill Carlisle liked it and I worked two years with him and played on a lot of his records. Then I got on with Porter Wagoner." The distinctive ring of Buck's twangy electric five string banjo was featured on many of Wagoner's hit songs and the early hits of the girl singer who joined the show in 1965, Dolly Parton.

Buck's credits also include being a regular on the top rated TV series "Hee Haw", being among the first Country entertainers to perform in the Soviet Union (with Roy Clark), winning awards from the Country Music Association for his instrumental albums with Clark and years of weekly appearances in The Porter Wagoner TV show.

After traveling the world, Buck has found a home in Branson. But it didn't happen all at once. It started with a one night stand at the Baldknobbers in 1971. Over the past 25 years Buck has performed at over ten venues in the Branson area. "In 1981 through 1983, because I had been a regular on Hee Haw, a bunch of us ... Lulu Roman, Archie Campbell, George Lindsey and all ... appeared at the Hee Haw Theater where Mickey Gilley's is now. That's when I got to really look around. There was zero crime. That was good. But I learned that waitresses could make or break you. If they liked your show they could recommend you to their customers. If they didn't like you they could sink you.

"In '87 I went to work for Chisai Childs at her theater where Bart Rockett is now. That's when we actually moved to Branson. In '88 Barbara Fairchild and I worked with Lowe's where Jim Stafford is now. Then I opened for Mickey Gilley in 1990. We did two shows a day, seven days a week for six months. That's when the season ran from April to October and we had to get all we could in those months.

"Then I opened the first morning show at the Pantry down by Fall Creek. Then we went to Crockey's south of Hollister ... then Pump Boys Theater ... and on to Jim Stafford's and Anita Bryant's ... and in 98 we did breakfast and show at the Dinner Bell. I was there for 7 years."

Today Buck does the morning show at Grand Country Music Hall where he takes time to visit with guests at the Grand Buffett before and after the show.

"It don't get no better than Branson. It's like Moe Bandy said, 'Now you can get to put your socks in the drawer'. I don't have to go out on the road. It's all right here: My outfits, instruments, the sound. the lights. I just get up, go to work, do the show and go home ... play golf or do whatever it is I want to do."

Jim Owen

JIM OWEN

Jim Owen's entertainment career has been multi-faceted: Hit songwriter, entertainer, show producer and award winning Hank Williams tribute artist.

And driving all that is a passion for the history of Country Music and its legendary entertainers.

Each year Jim's shows are built around another Country Music legend: Johnny Cash, Ernest Tubb, Hank Snow, Eddy Arnold, Mel Tillis, etc.. Many of them he knew personally, "In fact I worked one time as a songwriter for Mel Tillis' publishing company until he fired me. He built a new patio next to his home an wouldn't quit bragging about it. It really got on my nerves. So one weekend when he was out of town I turned a bunch of ducks loose on his new patio. They turned the patio into a 'potty-o'. Monday when he got back to town he fired me."

Jim's Branson career began in 1991 after an 8 year run in Las Vegas portraying Hank Williams in Legends in Concert. A group called The Texans dedicated half their show to some of the legendary acts in Country Music featuring guests like Freddie Hart, Ernie Ashworth, Charlie Louvin, George Hamilton IV, Jean Shepard and Jim doing his tribute to Hank Williams.

From there Jim began his own show at the Branson Mall Theater, then on to Pump Boys and Dinettes' Theater and later settling for a while at the Mickey Gilley theater.

"One day while I was at Gilley's I was doing a song called 'A Woman to Lean On' that I had written and Charley Pride had recorded. As I began the song Charley walked in from the side of the stage, grabbed my mike, sang the rest of the song and walked off stage. I didn't even know he was in the theater. He disappeared without saying a word. What a surprise!

Don Paul Pirwitz

"One thing about being in Branson is the opportunity to get close to the audience. I begin each show actually in the audience, I spend about 20 minutes visiting with the folks and answering questions. To make it in Branson you have to be willing to get close to the people."

One of Owen's greatest claims to fame is his songwriting. Over the years he's written hit songs for Tillis and Jim Ed Brown but his biggest hit is undoubtedly "Louisianna Woman Mississippi Man", a song that sold millions for Conway Twitty and Loretta Lynn and was named by Country Music Television as the second biggest Country duet of all time. "I wrote it for Conway and Loretta but I was under contact to RCA and was obligated to give first refusal to Porter Wagoner and Dolly Parton. I didn't see them doing justice to the song so I waited for a day when I knew Porter would be in a real fowl mood and brought him the song. He turned it down and I was free to pitch it to Conway and Loretta."

Jim also tells the story of a song he didn't write, didn't sing but did inspire. It happed one night while he was driving one of his classic cars, a Cadillac, between Nashville and Cincinnatti enroute to a date to do his Hank Williams Tribute show. "I picked up a hitchhiker. As we drove along he got to looking at some pictures I had laying on the seat of me as Hank. He kept looking at the pictures and looking at me. I could tell what he was thinking and did everything I could to help him think what he was thinking. I stopped for gas just outside Cincinnatti and this kid took off like a shot. Later I was doing a movie as Hank and Gary Gentry was playing guitar as one of the Drifting Cowboys. I told him the story and as a result he wrote 'The Ride', a song about a hitchhiker being picked up by the ghost of Hank Williams, which turned out to be a big hit for David Alan Coe. I had the chance to record it before David Alan but my producer at the time said 'No, you've done enough stuff about Hank'."

BRANSON FACTS

According to the Branson Lakes Area Chamber of Commerce ....

Over 7-million visitors come to Branson each year.

Most (about 65 percent) are adults or seniors. The rest (about 35 percent) come as families.

The average age of visitors is just over 57 years.

The average stay is 3 to 4 nights.

Most (over 31 percent) come in the summer, 20 percent come in the fall (September-October), 20 percent come during the holiday season (November-December), just over 18 percent come in the spring and nearly 10 percent come in winter.

Most (over 62 percent) come from outside of a 300 miles radius of Branson, just over 20 percent travel between 100 and 300 miles and nearly 20 percent come from within 100 miles of the city.

Branson boasts 47 theaters which are home to over 100 shows. There are close to 60,000 seats.

There are over 200 hotels, motels, lodges, etc. with nearly 18,000 rooms.

The city has over 400 restaurants with over 35,000 seats.

The population of Branson (according to the 2000 census) is 6050.

Tim Hadler

THE LAST HANK

For entertainer Tim Hadler it's all about being close to the fans.

His day starts at 5:30 in the morning. Following Bible study, family time and a big breakfast of eggs, bacon and hash browns, he's off to the hotels. By 7, armed with his guitar and Stetson hat he's in the breakfast rooms, giving impromtu performances and inviting folks to his 5pm show at the Little Opry Theater in the IMAX Entertainment Complex. By 8:30 he's moved on to major restaurants in the Branson area: Cracker Barrel, Shoney's, Denny's and McFarlan's.

The show is called "Hank Williams Revisted" and features Hank's songs and others done in the traditional Williams style with basic lead guitar, steel guitar, upright bass and rythmn guitar.

Tim remembers growing up in the 70's and 80's on the family's dairy farm in Washington State. "I was the youngest of 9 kids. I would be up early, milking and listening to KVAN in Vancouver. They would play the current hits, back then it was Willie Nelson and George Jones as well as classics by Ernest Tubb and Hank Williams. I loved the way Hank sang and I got to going through my dad's record collection and finding a real treasure of Hank's songs. I got to reading about Hank and thought: Hey, that's Hank Jr.'s daddy. I was hooked.

"I went to Nashville and started doing a Hank tribute show at some of the night clubs in Music City: The Wild Horse Saloon, Nashville Palace and Tootsie's Orchid Lounge." A high point came when he was invited to sing on the Grand Ol' Opry. "Stonewall Jackson introduced me on stage. His introduction lasted over a minute. He really made me feel important."

Don Paul Pirwitz

It was backstage at the Opry Tim observed the value that was put on contact with the fans. "Back then, if you were backstage, you could go just about anywhere. Roy Acuff always had his dressing room door open, so did Grandpa Jones. They always had time to visit with anyone who stopped by. There was no 'I'm a big star so leave me alone' attitude. That concern for the fans seems to be a big part of the way things are done in Branson.

"I also got to be on The Crook and Chase Show on the Nashville Network. I got to open for Little Jimmy Dickens."

It was in 2002 when Tim came to the attention of Branson Show Producer Jerry Lee. "He invited me to come to Branson as part of his 'Country Tradition' show. I asked him, 'where is this Branson place?'. I had heard of it but didn't know that much about it." Another member of the Country Tradition cast was Michele Inskeep, also known as Aunt Edna. "She's with me today on 'Hank Williams Revisited' doing Patsy Cline songs and comedy."

Although Tim's wife, Angie and children Paul, Savannah, Austin and David all make appearances on the show, 2005 held some special moments. "Paul and Savannah took up regular spots on the show. Paul was 8 ... going on 20. He does some comedy and singing, Savannah is a clogger ... she's 6. When she was younger she took up clogging and announced that by the time she was 13 she wanted to be on the show. I was doing a show in Columbia, Missouri and she came along. She brought along her clogging shoes without me knowing it. I let her perform on the show I was surpised how good she was and now she's a regular.

"My family is a big part of what I've been able to do. My mom and dad, brothers and sisters, wife and kids have all given me support in the good times and the bad."

BRANSON TIME LINE

1894   Marvel Cave opens to tourists.

1958   Table Rock Dam completed, creating Table Rock Lake.

1959   The Baldknobbers open Branson's first show in the city's downtown .

1960   The Herschend family opens Silver Dollar City and Shepherd of the Hills Outdoor Theater opens in its present location.

1967   Presleys build the first theater on 76 highway.

1983   Roy Clark becomes the first international star to put his name on a Branson marquee.

1991   CBS "60 Minutes" features a segment on Branson, accelerating the "Branson boom".

1992   Grand Palace, Branson's largest theater, opens.

1995   Showboat Branson Belle launched on Table Rock Lake.

1999   Miss U. S. A. pageant telecast from the Grand Palace.

2001   Highway 65 becomes the first four-lane road to Branson.

2003   Celebration City theme park opens.

2006   Branson Landing opens on the shores of Lake Taneycomo.

Jim Stafford

JIM STAFFORD

Over the years I've seen performances by many of the world's most highly rated entertainers, Elvis Presley and Garth Brooks among them. Being a practical person I've always tried to reason what exactly it is that an entertainer is supposed to do for an audience. I still don't know exactly what that is but I strongly suspect no one does it any better than Jim Stafford.

During the Branson boom in the early 90s I had the opportunity to spend 13 weeks during one summer co-producing "Branson U. S. A.", a radio show from Silver Dollar City's Riverfront Playhouse hosted by Jim.

The show was a mix of music, comedy and storytelling. It pictured Branson as an idyllic little town tucked away in the Ozarks that just happened to also be the home of some of America's greatest entertainers. The guest list was impressive: Glen Campbell, Willie Nelson, Merle Haggard, Moe Bandy, John Davidson, just to name a few. Entertainers I could never have dreamed would be on our little radio show were willing to tear down their stages and move instruments, band members, parts of their sound systems to the stage at Silver Dollar City for twenty minutes on the air with us. The secret ingredient was Jim Stafford.

Jim had not only become aquainted with these celebrities during his Hollywod career as supervising writer on the Smothers Brothers televison show but he and his wife Ann were among the first to welcome these newcomers to town. I remember hearing how the Staffords sent sandwiches to Willie Nelson and his crew when they were rushing to get their new show into his theater and were just too busy to stop and go out for dinner.

Jim Stafford grew up in Eloise, Florida where his family owned the local dry cleaners and his dad, Woody, would entertain the neighbors from his front porch. "We lived on a deadend street close to a grocery store. My dad liked to sit on the porch, pick his guitar and sing. People would listen to him as they walked by, sometimes they'd just wave, sometimes he'd draw a small crowd. He loved making music but he never quite had the nerve to go all the way and make a career of it. But he knew a lot of the local musicians and I got to spend a lot of time around them."

In 1983 Jim made his first trip to Branson. "That's when Roy Clark opened his theater and I decided I wanted to move to Branson. I'd been on the road for close to 20 years and this seemed like a great place to settle down. I didn't quite know how to pull it off, but I was committed to the idea. In 1990 I got with Linda Wilson at the Wildwood Flower and began doing shows there. Later we moved to what is now the Caravelle Theater. We put up a marquee that looked like the neck of a guitar. Then we bought the theater next door and had a crane move the guitar neck to the front of the new theater.

"I've had some interesting people come see our show over the years. I met the man who was in charge of burying the dead in Normandy toward the end of World War II. One time a man came up to me and said 'I know you've never seen me but probably know who I am.' He was the cop who arrested Lee Harvey Oswald in a Dallas movie theater after the assassination of President Kennedy. He showed me a scar where the hammer of Oswald's gun had cut into his hand when he went to disarm him."

The Jim Stafford Show is full of surprises. A UFO floating off the stage and over the audience, a giant fish swimming above the audience during intermission along with Jim's world class finger pickin' guitar, comedy, a touch of magic and songs like "Spiders and Snakes", "Cow Pati" and "My Girl Bill" that have become familiar favorites over the years.

Then there's Jim's pride and joy ... the kids: Shea and G G.

"This year I went back on the road for the first time in 16 years. I took the kids with me. G G got to celebrate her 9th birthday backstage at the Orleans Hotel in Las Vegas. That was really special.

"They were each just a few days old when they first appeared on stage. They often argue about who was the youngest when they started. Today they each have a regular part in the show. G G plays piano and banjo, Shea plays drums, fiddle, piano and whatever he can get his hands on. We see that they keep up on their lessons. Sometimes they complain but if someone comes over to the house and we get to talking about something new they're working on they'll race each other to the piano to show it off."

Amanda

AMANDA

Amanda Haffeke practically grew up on the Branson stage.

At age 9 she auditioned for Positive Country, a show in what is now the Pierce Arrow Theater on Shepherd of the Hills Expressway. When she was offered the job her family didn't hesitate to move two hundred miles from their home in Kirksville, MO. It meant that her dad would have to quit his job with a local electric company, they would have to sell their home, pack up, look for a new home in Branson and her dad would have to find a new job in the Ozarks,. It was all accomplished within a month.

Later she worked for Chisai Childs on her Branson Spotlight Show. Chisai got her an audition for Bob Wehr and his Branson U. S. A. show.

"I didn't think he was going to like me because I was just a kid," Amanda recalls. "But I sang 'Unchained Melody'. I found out later it was his favorite song. I got the job."

Soon after, Wehr sold his theater to make way for Celebration City and moved to what had been The Charley Pride Theater. The showplace, located on a hilltop about a half mile south of 76 Country Boulevard, was renamed The White House Theater and show called The Magnificent Seven Show because the cast was made up of 7 entertainers. The cast grew and the name had to be altered: It became The Magnificent 7 *PM* show.

The show features a cast of 10 singer-dancers, a versatile band, a dazzling rainbow of colorful costumes and an eclectic mix of music from Country to pop to big band and Latin.

Don Paul Pirwitz

Amanda's favorite part of the show: "The swing dance set. I got to be part of a lot of 'lifts'. I guess it's because I'm small and easy to lift."

One of her biggest on stage thrills: "Getting to sing with Country star Colin Raye on a Showcase Jubilee TV special."

A typical day during her High School years: Getting up early and working out, off to school at Branson High, show rehearsals after school, show in the evening and, somewhere along the way, homework and extra-curricular activites. "I was an officer in the Future Business Leaders of America, in the Fellowship of Christian Athletes, Public Relations person for the Young Republicans ... and few more things."

Did she consider herself a typical teenager? "Yes and no. During the day I was pretty normal for my age. I went to a public school. But at night I lived in the adult world on a year round show. But sometimes on Saturday nights I'd have a sleepover with some of my friends and my younger brother and I built a paintball fort near our new home."

Future plans involve college and pursuing a national recording career.
"Someday I'd like to open a dance club in Springfield. I'd have a house band during the week and perform there on weekends."

And in her spare time: "I like keeping busy. I don't like spare time."

USED TO BE'S

If you return to Branson after several year's absence, you may find some of the theaters you knew missing. Well, chances are they're still there under new names.

- The White House Theater used to be The Charley Pride Theater.
- Mansion America used to be The Magical Mansion and before that the Wayne Newton Theater.
- The Yakov Smirnoff Theater used to be The Will Rogers Theater, and before that, the second Mel Tillis Theater.
- The Follies Theater used to be The Glen Campbell Good Time Theater.
- The Duttons' Theater used to be The Boxcar Willie Theater and before that, The Wilkinson Brothers' Theater..
- The Tri-Lakes Center used to be the third Mel Tillis Theater.
- The Mickey Gilley Theater now stands where Bill and Janet Daily's Country Music World used to be, and before that, The Hee Haw Theater.
- The Jim Stafford Theater used to be the Lowe's Theater.
- Caravelle Theater used to be the Jim Stafford Theater.
- The Hughes Brothers Celebrity Theater used to be The Roy Clark Celebrity Theater.
- The Legends Theater used to be The Osmonds' Family Theater, The Texans Theater and first opened as Bob o Links (founded by Bob Mabe who used to be one of the original Baldknobbers).
- The Country Tonight Theater used to be the Moe Bandy Americana Theater and originally The Plummer Family Theater.
- The Bart Rocket Theater used to be Jimmy Osmond's American Jukebox Theater, The Christy Lane Theater and before that The Chisai Child's Starlight Theater.
- The theater at the bottom of the hill behind the Olive Garden restaurant on 76 Country Boulevard used to be the Kirby Van Birch, Yakov Smirnoff, Willie Nelson/Merle Haggard, the first Mel Tillis and first Shoji Tabuchi Theater.

I'm sure this list is not complete.

I'm also pretty sure we will never say " …. used to be The Baldknobbers's Theater" or …"used to be the Presley's Theater".

Terry Sanders

AKA HOMER LEE

When he was 6 years old Terry Sanders traveled with his family to Silver Dollar City. He was impressed. So impressed that when he returned to his home in Mountain Grove, MO he built his own version of Silver Dollar City in his back yard. "I made it from scrap lumber," he says, "I had a general store, blacksmith shop, museum and a three story tree house. It was pretty crude but tens of people from the neighborhood came to see it."

In 1980 Terry returned to Silver Dollar City on board Rube Dugan's Diving Belle. "I would seat people in the craft but I wanted it to be more than just a ride. I wanted it to be a show." Soon the then-mayor of Silver Dollar City, Shad Heller, invited Terry to be a part of his Corn Crib Theater Show.

From there it was on to the Wilkinson Brothers' Show, the Braschlers and Grand Jubilee at Grand Country Music Hall. Through it all Terry maintained his presence at Silver Dollar City. He also took a job at Branson's Vacation Channel as Terry The Tour Guide, introducing viewers to various attraction around the area.

It was while working with the Wilkinson Brothers he developed his best known character, Homer Lee. "Homer Lee is sort of a maintenance man or parking attendant who really wants to force his way on stage. He was inspired by Branson Comedians Herkimer and Droopy Drawers as well as Jerry Lewis, Judy Canova and Bugs Bunny. I always enjoyed Bugs ... he was always the center of attention and he never minded dressing up like a woman if it helped him get out of a jam."

Being in drag is also a part of Terry's act. He portrays over 35 characters including 104 year old Grandma Beulah and Joan Rivers. "When the Herschends opened Dixie Stampede. They invited me to come to a party at their home for Dolly Parton. I was asked to help host the party as Joan Rivers. It was fun. I got to hang out with Dolly for the evening. She was delightful ... totally without pretense."

The high point of his career: "Doing 13 episodes as a regular on Hee Haw. My mom had terminal cancer at the time. I had just gotten married and now I'd made it to national television. I was glad she was able to see that I had actually grown up and made something of myself. Minnie Pearl was a cancer survivor at the time. She would call my mom and encourage her. Roy Clark and some of the other Hee Haw stars would call her from time to time. It was a real heart warming experience."

Today Terry's on stage home is with The Branson Brothers Show at the Bart Rockett Theater. He can still be seen as Terry the Tour Guide on The Vacation Channel and his sons, Austin and Evan perform alternately as Little Pete in the "Shepherd of the Hills" outdoor theater.

Christmas at Silver Dollar City

Doug Gabriel and his Mufftar

DOUG GABRIEL

Raised in a cabin with a dirt floor in the country east of Branson, Don Gabriel later moved to Chicago where he once witnessed a shootout between local gangsters and police. His life came full circle in 1985 when his son Doug moved to Branson and began performing there.

Doug Gabriel began singing in public at age 3. "At age 10 I got my first guitar," he recalls. "At 12 I formed a group called New Relations and began performing professionally.

"Our first show was at the pavilion at Jaywood Park in Iowa. We drew about 500 people. It was huge! They brought us back for a second show and drew another 500. We could have been big like Alabama but they got national attention first. Country singer Johnny Dollar produced an album with us. It was called 'Great Vibes with Mufftars'. A song from the album, 'Highway 41', strangely enough made it to number 41 on the CASHBOX record chart. We once played The Louisiana Hayride in Shreveport (The radio show billed as 'The Cradle of the Stars'. It gave first exposure to the likes of Elvis Presley, Hank Williams, Jim Reeves and Johnny Cash). They told us we were the first self contained group to play on the show without the Hayride Band. "

An early influence on young Doug was his uncle Al. "He had a group called Al Stanley and the Neutrons. He played around the Chicago area and was the first artist to play the guitar behind his head. A lot of folks associate that with Chuck Berry but my Uncle Al did it first. He took time to teach me to play guitar."

Doug's grandfather, Glen, first made him and his family aware of Branson. He lived in Nixa (about 25 miles north of Branson). "Back then the Presleys and Baldknobbers were about the only shows in town. After seeing their shows I loved Branson but at the time I wanted to pursue a national career"

Things changed. Branson broadened it's entertainment base and New Relations broke up. Doug finally made his way to the Branson stage thanks to Chisai Childs. "I had performed on her show in Grapevine, Texas and she invited me to audition for her show when she moved to Branson. The audition was in front of a live audience. I was scared to death but I got the job.

"Later my friend Steve Sifford called and said he was forming a quartet. We put the group together and auditioned for Jim Thomas, co-owner of the Roy Clark Celebrity Theater. He held the auditon in a bathroom. We liked the accoustics in there. After listening to us Jim said, 'You sound really good but I'm not sure we can get much of an audience in here'."

The group, known as Roys Boys and later The Celebrity Sounds, went from singing in the restroom to the stage of the Celebrity Theater. "We would open for some of the major names that were booked at the dinner theater. Roy Clark would headline many of the shows. The first time we performed for Roy he walked in in the middle of a show where we were doing a tribute to some of the legends of Country Music. I was doing Little Jimmy Dickens, wearing an oversized cowboy hat and playing an oversized guitar. I guess I looked pretty silly. Roy has never let me forget just how silly."

Doug and Roy formed a long term relationship. "After I left Roy's theater we kept in contact. Later I started my own show and eventually found myself performing mornings at the Legends in Concert Theater. I asked Roy if he would like to share the bill with me on selected dates. He agreed and for four years we were back on the same stage again."

Today Doug, his wife Cheryl and their three children, Josh, Jordan and Jasmine perform mornings at the Jim Stafford

Theater. Doug first saw Cheryl when she and her two sisters were singing in Church in Cedar Rapids. "I picked her out the first time I saw her. I knew I loved her." Later she performed with Doug's show.

One if the unique features of Doug's performance is the "mufftar", a guitar made out of a muffler. "My dad owned a Midas Muffler shop and built the thing. It's gotten us a lot of national attention. It was featured in PEOPLE Magazine."

Danny Eakin (right) with the Homestead Pickers

DANNY EAKIN

Silver Dollar City street entertainer Danny Eakin has made his mark on the entertainment scene worldwide. Not just for his instrumental prowess and singing but also for his ability to sound like a dog, mule, turkey or just about any animal that may have survived the flood on Noah's Ark.

His voice has been heard as part of the pre-show sound check at IMAX movie theaters around the globe. "Jim Stafford put the thing together and asked me if I could do all the animal sounds. I said, everything but a goat. I just never could do a goat. There was a harmonica player at the session and I said, 'get him to do it.' He said he'd never done a goat before but he tried and he got it right. It's something about the way a harmonica player has to breathe that gives them the ability to sound like a goat."

Danny learned his craft in the woods of Northwest Arkansas near his boyhood home in Booger Holler, just off Highway 7 about one hundred miles south of Branson. "I was a lonely, lonely boy. When I was 10 or 11 my mama got me a guitar. She asked me to sing in church once in a while. Lots of afternoons I would head out into the woods and found a place on an old stump where a spring came out of the hill. I would practice my guitar and as it got dark I could hear the coon hunters runnin' their dogs through a holler a ways off. Well, I loved the way the dogs sounded and I got to makin' my own dog sounds." From there he graduated to other animal sounds.

As the years went by Danny found himself working as a lounge singer working the Holiday Inn circuit. To look at him and talk with him it's just about impossible to picture this hillbilly (he proudly wears the title) in that role. "Oh yeah, I did the whole thing .... "Feelings', 'Killing Me Softly' ... all the John Denver songs ... and once in a while I'd bark. There was a place in Pennsylvania where several coon hunters heard me. The next

Don Paul Pirwitz

Saturday Night they brought a bunch of their buddies. They'd say, 'you just gotta hear this' and I'd end up doing a lot of dog sounds. It was kind of rough on my voice. But they loved it and my career took a whole new turn."

Danny first came to Silver Dollar City in 1985 by way of the Tri-Lakes Community Theater. "They were doing 'Once Upon a Mattress' adapted from the story of 'The Princess and the Pea' and I auditioned for the part of the traveling minstrel. Jim Moeskau from Silver Dollar City was producing the show. I was asked if I could do the part with a French accent. I said 'I'm sorry this is the only accent I got'. But anyway, Jim called Rex Burdett at Silver Dollar City and suggested he audition me to be a traveling minstrel there. So, I got to audition for him during rehearsals for the show, right there in curly toed shoes, tights and billowy underwear."

A highpoint of his career at Silver Dollar City came one summer day when he had finished his show on one of the small stages in the park. A line of fans had formed to buy Danny's tapes and pictures. "I looked back in the line and there was Jack Herschend (one of the founders of Silver Dollar City). I wondered what he wanted. He stayed in line and when he got to me I asked if I could help him with anything. He just said, 'I'm glad you're here. We love working with people like you. You're real.' That's why it's so great working for the Herschend family. They'll always tell you the truth and then hug your neck."

Today Danny performs with the Homestead Pickers, a four piece acoustic band that plays on the front porch of The old homestead just off the main square. "Once in a while the Hershends will serve dinner to special celebrity guests inside the little homestead building. Usually they'll serve fried chicken, taters and gravy and we get to pick for the group. We've entertained Mickey Rooney, Paul Harvey, Glen Campbell, Tony Orlando and a bunch of others inside that little building."

Occasionally, on Sundays, Danny can be found performing at churches around the Ozarks. "They ask me to do some of the gospel songs I grew up on, tell my story and, at least once during the performance, bark like a dog."

Yakov Smirnoff

YAKOV SMIRNOFF

When the Soviet Union collapsed it wasn't necessarily a good thing for Russian comedian Yakov Smirnoff. He remembers making David Letterman's top ten list of things that would change with the fall of the Soviet Union. "Number one was Yakov Smirnoff will be out of work. I was known to many as a one joke comedian. The one joke was the Soviet Union.

"I didn't worry too much about it. But I noticed contracts began being cancelled or not renewed. I had two kids and a two-and-a-half million dollar home in Pacific Palisades and the bills kept coming in.

"I had been working Atlantic City, Las Vegas and places like that. My manager had told me about Branson and I had asked, 'Why Branson?'" With a change in his employment outlook Yakov made two trips to Branson.

"The first was kind of a business trip and it was okay. I saw Shoji Tabuchi playing to sell out crowds even in early March. Jim Stafford let me come out on stage with him and I could see that audience was quick to embrace me. I began to see the business potential here. On my second trip I took a taxi down from Springfield and the driver got lost. He ended up taking me across Table Rock dam, I got a good look at the lake and I said 'I can have a business here and live like this?' The combination was really good."

Yakov's first shows were at Branson's biggest theater, the Grand Palace; then on to his own theater at the bottom of a hill at the west end of 76 Country Boulevard and finally to his present theater overlooking highway 65 just north of highway 248. It's the first theater most visitors see as they enter Branson from the north.

Don Paul Pirwitz

The Yakov Smirnoff show is more than just stand up comedy. "I have ten Russian dancers, a juggler ...Slim Chance, a sense of patriotism ... It's more of a total variety show ... my goal is to entertain."

Aside from the show, Yakov's presence in Branson has been marked by spectacular outdoor advertising. On the highway 248 side of his theater, a massive three-dimensional marquee shows the Russian comedian crawling through barbed wire with his upper half on one side and his legs, with moving feet on the other. When it was first erected years ago along 76 Country Boulevard, the motors used to drive the feet burned out, air conditioners had to be installed to cool them. Over the past couple of seasons, a series of billboards showed Yakov holding a stick of dynamite with a glowing fuse which got shorter as they neared Branson with a warning to expect "explosive comedy". The face of the theater is bathed each night with flashing red, white and blue floodlights.

The move to Branson has given Yakov a chance to grow into areas where he hadn't been before. "I do my own marketing and work personally with my staff. I run every aspect of the theater. I used to be just a guy who traveled but now I've become a more well rounded business man."

One priority for the Russian comedian is getting to meet the fans, either during intermission or after the show. "There are times when I've had to leave right away to catch a plane or something but I think it's an important part of being here. That's what Branson was and it ought to be that way. Las Vegas doesn't do it, Broadway doesn't do it. I don't know of anywhere else where celebrities choose to go out and meet the people."

One of the brightest moments in Yakov's Branson career came when a young service man approached him before the show. "He was getting ready to ship out and asked if he could propose to his girl friend on the show. And I said 'sure, I'd like that'. She didn't know about it. He came out on stage and asked her to marry him. It was really special."

During a recent visit Yakov introduced me to a new passion that has taken him from the Branson stage to a smaller classroom style environment . "It's an interactive presentation on love and laughter. It's sort of a correlation between the two. It's what I want to be remembered for ... my legacy. I want to go from being strictly a Russian comedian to being more of a funny philosopher."

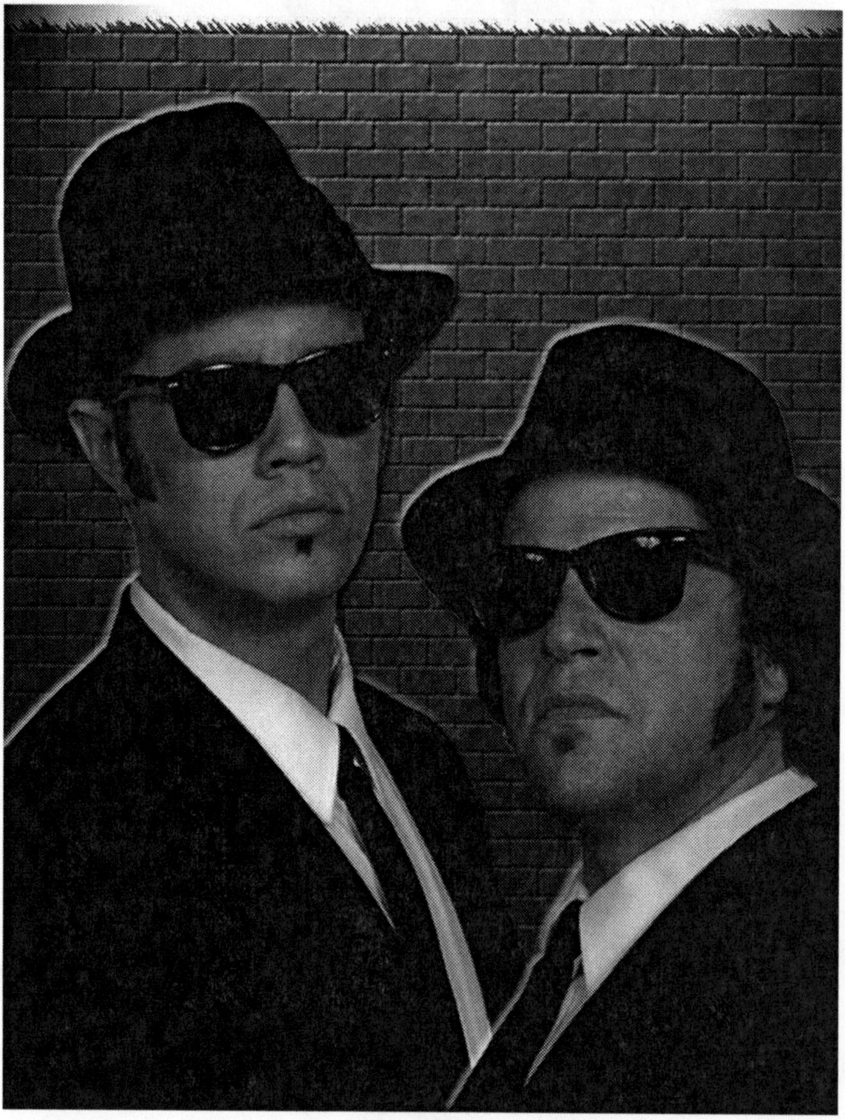

LEGENDS IN CONCERT

One marquee along 76 Country Boulevard boasts more star power than any other. At any one time it may advertise appearances by Elvis Presley, Shania Twain, Garth Brooks, The Blues Brothers, Buddy Holly, Dolly Parton or one of dozens of other superstars. The show is Legends in Concert.

Although the performers are not what you might call the real thing, they what some might call impersonators or, as they prefer, tribute artists: paying tribute to the stars they represent.

The show is spectacular with dazzling lighting and video effects, dancers and live band. An off stage voice is quick to point out that the artists use their own natural voices.

Legends mainstays Justin Clark and Bucky Heard perform as The Blues Brothers. They are quick to point out that their performance is more demanding than those of the real performers in that they need to pack into fifteen minutes what their counterparts in the real world take up to an hour to deliver. As evidence of the physical stress they're under the duo points to past injuries suffered during the intense dancing/acrobatics that are a part of their set.

Don Paul Pirwitz

Stacy Whitton as Marilyn Monroe

Stacy Whitton has been with Legends for over a dozen years performing tributes to Shania Twain and Marilyn Monroe, sometimes doing both during the same show.

Is it difficult performing as two such different personalities? "It's all a wig thing", Stacy reveals. "I guess it's all psychological, but I wear wigs for each character and the wig helps me create the character. After a while it tends to come natural ... the facial expressions and all.

"Between Shania and Marliyn I get to express my musical side and my comedy side. I guess I'm actually more like Shania in certain ways. Although I did hear her say once that she didn't really enjoy being on stage that much but preferred writing and making records. I love being on stage! And when I perform as Stacy Whitton, doing my own songs, I don't sing anything like Shania.

"I find Marilyn a lot more interesting. I think she and I had a lot in common in that, like me, she was always struggling to be taken seriously. I found it easy to sing like her but it took me two to three months to learn to talk like her. She had a funny ... I guess you would call it a dialect. She tended to over-pronounce her words. I studied all her movies and I would read magazines into a tape recorder in order to get her dialect down."

One of her most daring segments during the show is taking a man out of the audience and bringing him on stage with her. "I look for someone wearing glasses and I take his glasses off and put them down the front of my dress. After I'm through with him I reach in, get the glasses and give them back to him. There have been times when I haven't been able to find the glasses or one of the lenses fall out. That's kind of embarassing."

Stacy has performed as Shania and Marilyn not only in Branson but also at Legends in Las Vegas, Myrtle Beach, Singapore, Australia, Toronto and Japan. "We did a show once in Diego Garcia. I said I needed to cancel because I was getting married. The company was good enough to let me bring my husband along so we could honeymoon there and still do the show."

One night in Las Vegas she played to any unexpected guest. "As I was going on stage to do Shania someone told me she was in the audience. I knew they were kidding so I wasn't particularly nervous. After the show she came back to my dressing room and said she had enjoyed the show."

Don Paul Pirwitz

Doug Brewin as Alan Jackson

Legends artist Doug Brewin is from the South ... South Jersey that is.

His career began with performances in a wedding band with his sister and a couple of friends. "We found we were competing for jobs with DJs and made it a point to sound as much as possible like the records of the pop songs we were doing. I wasn't singing Country back then but I could do a pretty good Elton John."

Later he formed a band called Late Night Rodeo and played clubs around New Jersey. When he's not performing with Legends in Branson or Las Vegas he can most likely be found at Prospector's in Mount Laurel. "In 2004 we were performing at a special party for the Professional Bull Riders Association following one of their events at Balley's Wild West in Atlantic City. We were doing some Alan Jackson songs and one of the guys in the audience told the entertainment director there, 'I can't believe you got Alan Jackson for us.' I knew Alan's music but I didn't really know what he looked like. So I went to the mall and checked out some of his CDs. Meanwhile, the entertainment director at Balley's told the production manager at Legends about me and I got an audition. Well, anyway, here I am."

In early 2006, Doug made an appearance at the MGM Grand in Las Vegas while the Billboard Music Awards were going on. "It was kind of a stunt and I wasn't totally aware of what was going on. They drove me up to the front of the hotel in a Hummer stretch limo. They had three security guys and a couple of TV cameras follow me as I strolled through the casino and exited down the red carpet in the back. Lots of people asked for autographs. I DID sign them 'Doug Brewin'. I felt kind of uneasy about the whole thing. I was afraid Alan would find out and be angry about it. After it was over I got an interview on Inside Edition. When we got back to Jersey they played a video of the interview on some big screen TVs at Prospector's while we did the Brad Paisley song 'Celebrity'."

And what does the real Alan Jackson think of all this? "Well, a buddy of mine's mom is best friends with Alan's mom. She said when he found out about my act he felt good about it ... said he didn't think he was legend enough to be worthy of a tribute like this."

Shoji Tabuchi

SHOJI TABUCHI

Go figure! Over the years Branson has seen superstars come and go: Johnny Cash, Willie Nelson, Merle Haggard, Wayne Newton. And yet one of Branson's consistent top entertainers is an otherwise (nearly) unknown Japanese fiddler: Shoji Tabuchi.

The Shoji Tabuchi show is big! Perhaps Branson's biggest with a cast of over 40 supported by an additional 40 sound, lighting, special effects and wardrobe people.

The show opens with a battery of Japanese drums including a centerpiece 8 foot Taiko drum. Before its end the audience is dazzled with a small army of dancers, backup singers and band. And at the center of it all, Shoji with his fiddling and disarming difficulty with the English language. "I used to live in Louisiana ... that's why I talk this way," he explains.

The young Shoji, an aspiring concert violinist, became enamored with country music when he a attended a concert featuring Roy Acuff and fiddler Howdy Forester. The clincher was Forester's version of "Listen to the Mocking Bird". He began playing country music began formulating a plan to move to the United States over the objections of his businessman father. "I waited until he was out of town ... and then I left the country".

Shortly after coming to America the young immigrant landed two jobs in Wichita, Kansas: by day as a hospital orderly and by night and on weekends as a fiddler in the KFDI Wichita Lineman band.

I first met Shoji a few years later in Philadelphia where he was working with Country star David Houston. It was a real novelty, a Japanese fiddler in a country band. Since he was having difficulty with the English language he had to learn to sing several songs phonetically with little or no knowledge of what the words meant.

Shoji's career then led to the Dallas area and the Grapevine Opry owned by another Japanese entertainer, Chisai Childs. Actually, Chisai was born in Tokyo of American parents and grew up in Texas.

When Chisai moved her show to Branson Shoji was invited to come along. He was an immediate hit. After a subsequent gig at Bill and Janet Dailey's Country Music World, Shoji opened his own show at a theater on the western part of 76 Country Boulevard backing up to Green Mountain Drive that subsequently housed the Mel Tillis show, Willie Nelson and Merle Haggard as well as Yakov Smirnoff and Kirby Van Birch.

The story goes that Shoji and Mel Tillis negotiated the transfer of the showplace. After hours of labored communication between the Japanese fiddler, struggling with the english language, and Tillis, trying hard to make himself understood through his famous stutter, there came a long pause, after which Shoji ended the conversation with "sold!!".

Shoji then took up residence at his new theater on Shepherd of the Hills Expressway. Two of the legendary features of the new facility are the ornate rest rooms: the ladies room complete with fresh flowers and full working fireplace and the men's room with its own billiard table.

Boxcar Willie

BOXCAR WILLIE

When I first met Boxcar Willie I had him figured as a 12-carat phony.

He was in Springfield producing an album at a local studio. Boxcar and his manager, Jim Martin, explained that although we had never heard of him here in the United States he was a big deal in the British Isles (like I was going to be able to affirm or discredit that).

You can imagine the amazement I felt when I was having my shoes shined some week's later, picked up a copy of PEOPLE magazine and came across a picture of Boxcar, his wife and family lounging beside the pool at their home in Texas.

At about the same time he appeared on the nationally televised "Gong Show". The show featured off beat entertainers. Some of them were really bad. The trick was to make it through a performance without being "gonged" ... having one of the three celebrity judges strike a large Chinese gong. Once an artist finished, he or she was given a score ... 1 through 10 ... by each of the judges. Not only did Boxcar not get gonged, he scored a perfect 10 with each of the judges. a feat rarely, if ever, done before or since.

Several years later, after Boxcar settled in Branson. I was giving a tour of the city to someone recently arrived from England. As we drove past the Boxcar Willie Theater, my guest asked, "Does Boxcar Willie perform in that place?" I confirmed that he did. "You know where he plays in England?" I confirmed that I didn't. "In big arenas, before tens of thousands of people."

Even though he never had a hit record Boxcar Willie became one of the most recognized artists in Country Music with his hobo persona and trademark train whistle.

Don Paul Pirwitz

On an episode of the sit-com "Seinfeld" Jerry referred to a homeless boyfriend of the character Elaine as "Boxcar Willie". I doubt that he could have made such an immediate point by dropping the name of many country music superstars.

Lecil Martin was born in Texas. As a child he was facinated by the sound of the whistles on the trains as they passed near the Martin home. The youngster learned to mimic the trains, even differentiating between the sounds the various engines made.

After an extended tour of duty with the U. S. Air Force, Martin made his move on Country Music. Using the name Marty Martin he scored a couple of fairly insignificant chart records and earned a place of the WWVA Wheeling Jamboree. Yet, his career was going nowhere. He needed a gimmick.

One day while driving near a rail yard a friend spotted a hobo and commented, "Well, there's ol' Boxcar Willie." A light went on somewhere about Lecil Martin's head. America's favorite hobo was born.

His career led him to membership in the prestegious Grand Ol' Opry, millions of records sold via a unique TV marketing campaign and a touring schedule that included appearances at The Roy Clark Celebity Theater in Branson. Across from the Clark Theater a showplace owned by the Wilkinson Brothers had a For Sale sign on it.

One night Boxcar called home and told his wife, Lloene, "Pack up. We 're moving to Branson. I just bought a theater."

One Saturday night in 1996 I took some friends to see Boxcar Willie. They weren't what you would call hard core country music fans. But, asked what Branson show they would most like to see (It could have been Andy Williams, Tony Orlando, Wayne Newton or any of the small army of pop artists in Branson at the time). Their response: "Boxcar Willie".

I knew they would be impressed with Boxcar's high energy show, his wit, his colorful stories. But that night something wasn't quite right. Boxcar was more subdued.
If I didn't know better I would have guessed he had been drinking before the show. By the end of the show the response of the audience seemed to lift his spirits and he was more like his usual self. I talked to him briefly during the intermission. He said he was feeling a little tired. The following Tuesday he announced that he had been diagnosed with leukemia.

In 1997 Boxcar was given a unique honor. The Branson Board of Aldermen decided to re-name St. Limas Street Boxcar Willie Boulevard. Up to that point no street in the city had ever been named after an entertainer.

Late one night, a couple of years later, I got a phone call. It was from Boxcar's daughter. "Dad just died." she announced.

Near my home in Springfield there are several railroad lines. Throughout that night it seemed they were sounding their train whistles more than usual.